Teach Me... Everyday ENGLISH™

Volume 1

Written by Judy Mahoney
Illustrated by Patrick Girouard

Technology is changing our world. Far away exotic places have literally become neighbors. We belong to a global community and our children are becoming "global kids." Comparing and understanding different languages and cultures is more vital than ever! Additionally, learning a foreign language reinforces a child's overall education. Early childhood is the optimal time for children to learn a second language, and the Teach Me Everyday language series is a practical and inspiring way to teach them. Through story and song, each book and audio encourages them to listen, speak, read and write in a foreign language.

Today's "global kids" hold tomorrow's world in their hands. So when it comes to learning a new language, don't be surprised when they say, "teach me!"

The English language developed mainly from the Anglo-Saxon and Norman-French languages. Today, English is the most widely spoken language in the world. In many countries, it is either the native language or a secondary language. Over 350 million people speak English as their native language. It has a very large vocabulary with over 600,000 words, with new words being added every year.

Teach Me Everyday English
Volume One
ISBN 13: 978-1-59972-108-8
Library of Congress PCN: 2008902655

Copyright © 2008 by Teach Me Tapes, Inc.
6016 Blue Circle Drive, Minnetonka, MN 55343
www.teachmetapes.com

Book Design by Design Lab, Northfield, MN

Printed in the United States of America.

10 9 8 7 6 5 4 3 2

INDEX & SONG LIST

The More We Get Together

The more we get together, together, together
The more we get together the happier we'll be
For your friends are my friends and my friends are your friends
The more we get together the happier we'll be.

Hello!
My name is Marie.
What is your name?
This is my family.
my brother
my father
my mother
me
five

My cat.
Her name is Fluffy.
She is soft and gray.

my cat

My dog.
His name is Spot.
He is black and white.

my dog

My room is red.
It's seven o'clock.
Get up! Get up!

Are You Sleeping

Are you sleeping, are you sleeping
Brother John, Brother John
Morning bells are ringing
Morning bells are ringing
Ding dang dong! Ding dang dong!

Lazy Marie

Lazy Marie will you get up
Will you get up, will you get up?
Lazy Marie will you get up
Will you get up today?

Lazy Marie will you get dressed
Will you get dressed, will you get dressed?
Lazy Marie will you get dressed
Will you get dressed today?

Lazy Marie please brush your teeth
Brush your teeth, brush your teeth
Lazy Marie please brush your teeth
Please brush your teeth today.

Lazy Marie please wash your face
Wash your face, wash your face
Lazy Marie please wash your face
Please wash your face today.

Lazy Marie please make your bed
Make your bed, make your bed
Lazy Marie please make your bed
Please make your bed today.

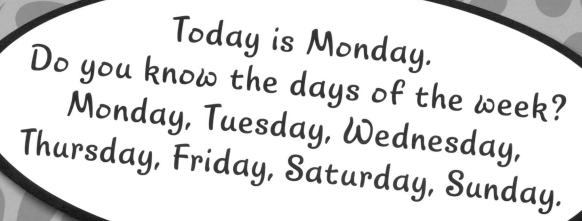

MONDAY

TUESDAY

WEDNESDAY

THURSDAY

FRIDAY

SATURDAY

SUNDAY

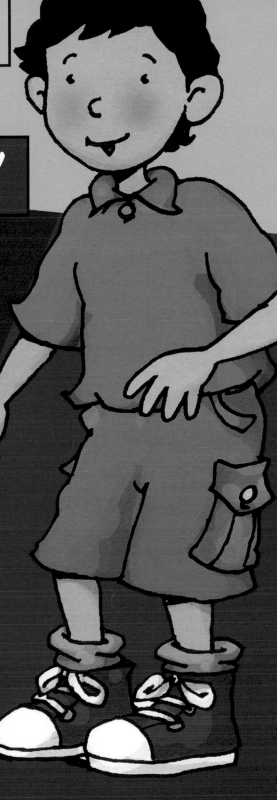

Rain Medley

Rain, rain, go away
Come again another day
Rain, rain, go away
Little Johnny wants to play.

It's raining, it's pouring
The old man is snoring
He bumped his head and went to bed
And couldn't get up in the morning.

Rainbows

Sometimes blue and sometimes green
Prettiest colors I've ever seen
Pink and purple, yellow-whee!
I love to ride those rainbows.

Here is my school. Today I will repeat the numbers and alphabet. Will you say them with me?

my school

NUMBERS

1 one 2 two 3 three 4 four 5 five 6 six 7 seven 8 eight 9 nine 10 ten

ALPHABET

Aa Bb Cc Dd
Ee Ff Gg
Hh Ii Jj Kk
Ll Mm Nn Oo Pp
Qq Rr Ss Tt Uu Vv
Ww Xx Yy Zz

Now I know my ABC's, next time won't you sing with me?

This Old Man

This old man, he played one
He played knick-knack on my thumb.

Chorus:
With a knick-knack paddy whack
Give a dog a bone
This old man came rolling home.

This old man, he played two
He played knick-knack on my shoe.
Chorus

This old man, he played three
He played knick-knack on my knee.
Chorus

This old man, he played four
He played knick-knack on my door.
Chorus

This old man, he played five
He played knick-knack on my hive.
Chorus

This old man, he played six
He played knick-knack on my sticks.
Chorus

This old man, he played seven
He played knick-knack up in heaven.
Chorus

This old man, he played eight
He played knick-knack on my gate.
Chorus

This old man, he played nine
He played knick-knack on my spine.
Chorus

This old man, he played ten
He played knick-knack once again.
Chorus

One Elephant

One elephant went out to play
Upon a spider's web one day
He had such enormous fun
That he called for another elephant to come.

Two...
Three...
Four...
All...

If You're Happy and You Know It

If you're happy and you know it
Clap your hands (clap, clap)
If you're happy and you know it
Clap your hands (clap, clap)
If you're happy and you know it
Then your face will surely show it
If you're happy and you know it
Clap your hands. (clap, clap)

If you're angry and you know it
Stomp your feet (stomp, stomp)
If you're angry and you know it
Stomp your feet (stomp, stomp)
It you're angry and you know it
Then your face will surely show it
If you're angry and you know it
Stomp your feet. (stomp, stomp)

If you're silly and you know it
Laugh out loud (giggle)
If you're silly and you know it
Laugh out loud (giggle)
If you're silly and you know it
Then your face will surely show it
If you're silly and you know it
Laugh out loud. (giggle)

If you're hungry and you know it
Rub your tummy (mmm, mmm)
If you're hungry and you know it
Rub your tummy (mmm, mmm)
If you're hungry and you know it
Then your face will surely show it
If you're hungry and you know it
Rub your tummy. (mmm, mmm)

If you're sleepy and you know it
Take a nap (sigh)
If you're sleepy and you know it
Take a nap (sigh)
If you're sleepy and you know it
Then your face will surely show it
If you're sleepy and you know it
Take a nap. (sigh)

The Puppets

Watch them hop, skip, jump
Oh, the puppets they can go
Watch them turn, fall, stand
You must not miss the show.

Can we still come back
To watch the puppets go
Can we still come back
Even when we are all grown.

The Wheels on the Car

The wheels on the car go round and round
Round and round, round and round
The wheels on the car go round and round
All around the town.

The horn on the car goes beep beep beep
Beep beep beep, beep beep beep
The horn on the car goes beep beep beep
All around the town.

The wipers on the car go swish swish swish
Swish swish swish, swish swish swish
The wipers on the car go swish swish swish
All around the town.

The lights on the car go blink blink blink
Blink blink blink, blink blink blink
The lights on the car go blink blink blink
All around the town.

The driver of the car says, "Buckle up"
"Buckle up, buckle up"
The driver of the car says, "Buckle up"
All around the town.

The children in the car say, "Let's have lunch"
"Let's have lunch, let's have lunch"
The children in the car say, "Let's have lunch"
All around the town.

After my quiet time, I go to the park to play. I like to feed the ducks. I sing and dance on the bridge with my friends.

On the Bridge of Avignon

On the bridge of Avignon
They're all dancing, they're all dancing
On the bridge of Avignon
They're all dancing round and round.

The Seasons Song

I like to rake the leaves
Into a big hump
Then I step back
Bend my knees and jump!

I like to make a snowball
And roll it on the ground
It grows into a snowman
So big and fat and round.

I am a little flower
My leaves are newly green
When you see my first bud
You know it's spring, it's spring!

It is now summer
The sun is shining bright
Our days are all our own
To stand and fly a kite.

Six Little Ducks

Six little ducks that I once knew
Fat ones, skinny ones, fair ones, too
But the one little duck
With the feather on his back
He led the others with his
Quack quack quack
Quack quack quack
Quack quack quack
He led the others with his
Quack quack quack.

Down to the river they would go
Wibble, wibble, wibble, wobble
All in a row
But the one little duck
With the feather on his back
He led the others with his
Quack quack quack.

Our Mother Earth

Our Mother Earth
It's our home
It's the only one we have.

Our Mother Earth
It's our home
We need to keep it clean.

The paper, the plastic
The glass should be recycled
It's you, it's me
Together we can save our earth.

I'm hungry!
It must be
time for dinner.

Oh! Susanna

Well, I come from Alabama
With a banjo on my knee
I'm goin' to Louisiana, my true love for to see
Oh, Susanna, won't you cry for me
'Cause I come from Alabama
With a banjo on my knee.

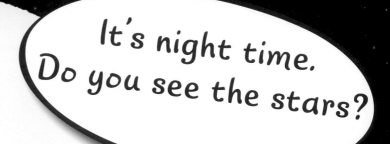

It's night time.
Do you see the stars?

Twinkle, Twinkle

Twinkle, twinkle, little star
How I wonder what you are
Up above the world so high
Like a diamond in the sky
Twinkle, twinkle, little star
How I wonder what you are!

Lullaby

Lullaby and goodnight
With roses delight
Creep into your bed
There pillow your head
If God will, you shall wake
When the morning does break
If God will, you shall wake
When the morning does break.

Lullaby and goodnight
Those blue eyes closed tight
Bright angels are near
So sleep without fear
They will guard you from harm
With fair dreamland's sweet charm
They will guard you from harm
With fair dreamland's sweet charm.

Want to learn more?

lamp

banjo

couch

ball

dog

pillow

window

bed

doll

hot cocoa

orange juice

bread

jam

tree

friend

bridge

soccer ball

COLORS

red

purple

blue

green

orange

gray

yellow

pink

brown

white

black